# Wealth Without Water

Matthew Petchinsky

1

# Wealth Without Water: The Post-Aquatic Rich Life

By: Matthew Petchinsky

**Disclaimer**

*Wealth Without Water: The Post-Aquatic Rich Life* is intended for educational, philosophical, and conceptual exploration only. This book presents metaphorical frameworks, symbolic language, and lifestyle perspectives designed to encourage personal reflection, mindset development, and creative thinking about wealth, sustainability, independence, and adaptation. It is not a substitute for professional advice of any kind.

Nothing in this book should be interpreted as financial, legal, medical, environmental, survivalist, engineering, investment, or business advice. The author does not provide guarantees of financial success, income generation, asset growth, or personal outcomes. Any references to wealth, prosperity, systems of value, or alternative lifestyles are illustrative and symbolic, not predictive or prescriptive.

Readers are solely responsible for their own decisions, actions, interpretations, and outcomes. Before making financial, legal, medical, environmental, or lifestyle changes—including those related to investments, resource management, relocation, health practices, or unconventional living models—readers should consult qualified professionals who can evaluate their specific circumstances.

This book uses imaginative and speculative language, including post-aquatic metaphors, adaptive wealth models, and abstract frameworks, to challenge conventional assumptions about scarcity, dependence, and value. These concepts are not literal instructions for survival without water, nor do they promote unsafe, harmful, or biologically impossible practices. Water remains essential for human life, and nothing in this book suggests otherwise.

Any case studies, scenarios, analogies, or examples are fictionalized, generalized, or symbolic. They are not representations of real individuals, organizations, or guaranteed paths to success. Past performance, hypothetical outcomes, or conceptual models discussed in this work do not indicate or promise future results.

The author makes no warranties, expressed or implied, regarding the completeness, accuracy, reliability, or applicability of the information contained herein. All content is provided "as is," and the author disclaims liability for any loss, injury, damage, or adverse outcome—financial, physical, emotional, environmental, or otherwise—that may result from the use or misuse of the material.

This book is intended for mature readers capable of critical thinking, discernment, and personal responsibility. By reading this work, you acknowledge that you are engaging with a conceptual framework designed to inspire thought, not to replace expertise, due diligence, or common sense.

If you do not agree with these terms, or if you require professional guidance, you should discontinue reading and seek appropriate expert assistance.

## Introduction

**No Water. No Problem. This Is Liquid-Free Capitalism.**

The first thing people assume when water disappears is that everything else must collapse with it.

Economies. Cities. Comfort. Wealth.

That assumption is wrong.

This book begins where that assumption fails.

*Wealth Without Water: The Post-Aquatic Rich Life* is not about denial, panic, or apocalyptic fantasy. It is about **adaptation**—financial, psychological, structural. When clean water becomes scarce, expensive, restricted, or weaponized, the old economic rules fracture. The people who cling to pre-scarcity thinking dehydrate financially long before their bodies do. The people who adapt early build power in the cracks.

This is a Q1–Q4 survival-finance manual for a future that is already arriving unevenly across the world. Not everywhere loses water at once. Not everyone loses it the same way. But the pattern is clear: access becomes tiered, controlled, monetized, and unstable. When that happens, wealth no longer flows like a river. It condenses, crystallizes, and migrates into new forms.

This book teaches you how to follow it.

You will not find doomsday prepping, fear-based hoarding, or survivalist machismo here. You will find **post-resource economics**—how income, leverage, and autonomy are created when a basic necessity can no longer be assumed. You will learn how to build value systems that do not depend on physical abundance, logistical stability, or institutional fairness.

Liquid-free capitalism does not mean ignoring reality. It means **designing around constraint**.

In a water-stressed world, labor shifts. Attention shifts. Infrastructure fractures. New gatekeepers emerge. Old careers evaporate. Entire industries dry up while others explode overnight. Those who understand this early stop chasing jobs that require stability and start building systems that thrive in volatility.

This book is structured to be evergreen—useful in Q1, Q2, Q3, and Q4—because scarcity does not follow calendar quarters. It pulses. It surges. It retreats and returns. So must your strategy.

You will learn how to:

- Create income streams that do not rely on physical supply chains
- Monetize knowledge, coordination, and perception rather than consumption
- Build wealth that survives environmental, political, and infrastructural stress
- Transition from dependency economics to adaptive sovereignty
- Thrive financially in environments where others are forced into desperation thinking

This is not about becoming rich *after* collapse. It is about becoming **anti-fragile before it**.

When water becomes unreliable, people panic. When people panic, they overpay, overreact, and surrender leverage. The post-aquatic rich do the opposite. They understand that scarcity does not erase value—it **rearranges it**. And those who understand the rearrangement early do not merely survive.

They accumulate.

No water. No problem.

This is not the end of wealth.

This is its next form.

# Chapter 1: Post-Water Economics

## The Hidden Assumption Beneath Every Economy

Every modern economy runs on an unspoken assumption: **continuity**.

Continuity of utilities.
Continuity of transport.
Continuity of institutions.

Most people never notice this assumption because it has held long enough to feel permanent. Water flows when the tap opens. Goods arrive when ordered. Money moves when tapped. Stability becomes invisible.

Post-water economics begins by exposing this dependency.

When clean water becomes unreliable—restricted, rationed, politicized, or priced beyond reach—the economic structures built on that assumption begin to fracture. This does not happen everywhere at once, and that delay is what traps most people psychologically. They wait for certainty. Operators move during ambiguity.

This chapter is not about panic or fantasy collapse. It is about **financial cognition under stress**—learning to think economically in conditions where continuity cannot be assumed.

**What Collapses First Under Scarcity**

Scarcity is selective.

It does not destroy everything. It **filters**.

The first economic systems to fail are those that require:

- Just-in-time logistics
- Daily physical presence
- Continuous utilities
- Regulatory stability
- Centralized permission

These systems fail not because they are poorly designed, but because they are **over-optimized for stability**.

Post-water economics asks a different question than traditional finance:

*What assumptions must remain true for this income to exist?*

If income collapses when any single assumption breaks, it is fragile by design.

**Scarcity Reassigns Value, It Does Not Erase It**

When water becomes unreliable, value moves upward—away from objects and toward **control, coordination, and interpretation**.

In scarcity conditions:

- Goods lose predictability
- Ownership becomes risky
- Transport becomes expensive
- Enforcement becomes uneven

Value migrates to those who:

- Control access
- Reduce uncertainty
- Coordinate outcomes
- Translate chaos into clarity

This is why operators outperform owners during stress. They do not need to possess resources. They **direct flow**.

### Why Abstract Assets Outlast Physical Infrastructure

Physical wealth feels solid in calm conditions. Under stress, it becomes heavy.

Every physical asset requires:

- Protection
- Movement
- Explanation
- Compliance

Abstract assets do not.

Skills travel without permits.
Knowledge scales without transport.
Coordination increases in value as systems fragment.

Post-water economics prioritizes:

- Intellectual leverage over inventory
- Roles over titles
- Systems over possessions

This is not detachment from reality—it is **friction reduction.**

**The Operator Class Emerges**

As infrastructure weakens, labor reorganizes.

Those who *execute tasks* lose leverage.

Those who *design outcomes* gain it.

Operators:

- Organize people who cannot find each other
- Interpret fragmented information
- Make decisions under constraint
- Build temporary order inside chaos

These roles expand during stress and scarcity. They do not require clean water, stable roads, or uninterrupted utilities. They require **clarity, trust, and timing**.

**Stress-Testing Wealth**

Post-water economics introduces a non-negotiable test:

**Would this income survive grid failure, rationing, or sanctions?**

If the answer is no, the income is **conditional**.

Conditional income is not useless—but it cannot be trusted alone.

Resilient income:

- Does not depend on daily physical infrastructure
- Is deliverable digitally or conceptually
- Cannot be easily shut down by a single authority
- Benefits from volatility rather than stability

This test permanently changes how wealth is evaluated.

**Dependency Economics vs Adaptive Sovereignty**
Traditional systems train dependency:

- One employer
- One location
- One platform
- One utility grid

Adaptive sovereignty replaces dependence with **optionality**. Sovereignty does not mean isolation. It means:

- Multiple income vectors
- Transferable skills
- Decision authority
- The ability to pivot without collapse

Under stress, dependent actors panic.
Sovereign actors reposition.

**Thriving While Others Panic**

Panic is caused by surprise, not scarcity.

Those who read patterns early:

- Exit before pressure peaks
- Accumulate positioning while others freeze
- Avoid premium pricing driven by fear

Post-water economics teaches **anticipatory intelligence**—the ability to see structural shifts before they dominate headlines.

This is not fear-based living.

It is **timing-based advantage**.

## Journal Prompts

1. What assumptions does my current income rely on that could break under environmental or political stress?
2. Which parts of my livelihood depend directly on clean water, stable utilities, or uninterrupted logistics?
3. If my primary income disappeared tomorrow, what skills would still hold value?
4. Where in my life am I dependent rather than sovereign?
5. What roles could I play that involve coordination rather than execution?
6. How do I personally react to instability—freeze, panic, or analyze?
7. What forms of wealth do I currently treat as "safe" without having stress-tested them?
8. Where have I already seen value shift during recent disruptions?
9. What would resilient income look like for me specifically?
10. What small step could I take this quarter to reduce my dependency on fragile systems?

## Closing Reflection

Post-water economics does not ask you to abandon society or fear the future. It asks you to **see clearly**.

Stability was never guaranteed—it was rented. And rent always comes due.

Those who thrive in volatile systems are not stronger, richer, or more ruthless. They are **less surprised**. They design their wealth to move, adapt, and survive pressure.

You are no longer learning how to earn inside a stable world.

You are learning how to **remain solvent inside an unstable one**.

This is not collapse thinking.

This is operator thinking.

And from here on, you build accordingly.

## Chapter 2: Bartering Brilliance

### The Myth of Primitive Barter

When people hear the word *barter*, they imagine something crude: two people exchanging objects in desperation, counting scarcity by hand. This image is wrong—and dangerously limiting.

Primitive barter is **object-for-object**.
Post-water barter is **value-for-outcome**.

In unstable environments, physical goods lose reliability. They spoil, attract risk, require protection, and draw attention. What replaces them is not chaos—it is **intelligence exchange**. Bartering evolves upward, not backward.

This chapter dismantles the idea that wealth requires possession and introduces **high-leverage bartering**, where the most valuable asset is not what you have, but **what you can align**.

**Why Information Outperforms Objects Under Stress**

In scarcity conditions, objects become heavy.

They must be:

- Stored
- Guarded
- Transported
- Justified
- Traded discreetly

Information does not.

Information:

- Moves instantly
- Replicates without loss
- Improves with context
- Scales without exposure

A person who knows *where*, *when*, and *how* something happens is more powerful than the person holding the thing itself. This is especially true when access is fragmented and certainty is rare.

Post-water bartering treats **knowledge as currency**, not commodity.

**Access Is the New Asset Class**

Ownership assumes stability.

Access thrives in instability.

When systems fracture, not everyone loses everything. Resources still exist—but they are unevenly distributed, gated, and confusing to reach. The person who knows **how to get something done** becomes indispensable.

Access includes:

- Knowing who to talk to
- Knowing how decisions are made
- Knowing timing windows
- Knowing informal channels
- Knowing which rules matter—and which don't

You do not need to own resources to trade access to them. You only need to be **trusted as a bridge**.

This is why brokers, fixers, translators, and coordinators gain power during scarcity. They reduce friction where others encounter walls.

**Coordination Is Scarcity's Most Valuable Skill**

Scarcity creates fragmentation.

People have pieces—but no picture.

Coordination turns fragments into outcomes. It is the ability to:

- Align incentives
- Reduce confusion
- Translate goals
- Synchronize effort

The coordinator does not need to supply goods. They **orchestrate movement**. In post-water economics, coordination becomes more valuable than production because production without alignment collapses.

This is where bartering evolves into **role-based leverage**.

You trade:

- Clarity for access
- Organization for compliance
- Timing for cooperation
- Structure for trust

No inventory required.

**Perception Becomes Currency**

In scarcity, trust is rare.

This makes perception **expensive**.

Reputation, credibility, and narrative control function as exchange multipliers. Two people offering identical information will not be valued equally. The one perceived as:

- Calm
- Reliable
- Consistent
- Neutral
- Competent

Receives disproportionate leverage.

Post-water bartering recognizes that **how you are perceived determines what your value converts into**. Trust compresses transaction costs. Distrust inflates them.

Your name, tone, and consistency become assets.

**Trading Outcomes Instead of Objects**
High-leverage barter does not trade items—it trades **results.** Examples include:

- Trading strategy instead of tools
- Trading verification instead of goods
- Trading organization instead of labor
- Trading interpretation instead of access

You might not provide water, food, or supplies. You might provide:

- Decision clarity
- Risk assessment
- Planning
- Conflict resolution
- System mapping

Outcomes are lighter than objects—and harder to replace.

**The Broker Advantage**

The broker does not compete with owners.

They **outperform them**.

Owners are limited by inventory. Brokers scale by relationships. The broker:

- Connects people who cannot find each other
- Facilitates exchange without exposure
- Extracts value from alignment
- Avoids possession risk

This role thrives without physical supply chains. Knowledge travels friction-free. Coordination compounds.

This is income without trucks, warehouses, or utilities.

**Adaptive Sovereignty Through Role, Not Possession**
Traditional power comes from ownership.
Post-water power comes from **position**.
Adaptive sovereignty is achieved when:

- You are difficult to remove
- Your role is portable
- Your value increases under stress
- Your absence creates disruption

Roles travel. Possessions anchor.

When you occupy a coordination role, people protect your access because you protect their outcomes.

This is sovereignty without stockpiles.

**The Barter Multiplier Effect**

Each successful exchange compounds credibility.

Credibility compounds perception.

Perception compounds access.

Access compounds opportunity.

This creates a feedback loop where:

- Less effort produces more value
- Fewer resources generate larger outcomes
- Your presence lowers friction

Bartering brilliance is not hustle. It is **leverage engineering**.

## Journal Prompts

1. What knowledge do I have that reduces confusion or risk for others?
2. Where do people already come to me for clarity or advice?
3. What resources do I not own but know how to access or align?
4. How am I currently undervaluing my ability to coordinate outcomes?
5. What reputation am I unintentionally projecting in stressful situations?
6. Which roles could I occupy that require trust rather than tools?
7. Where could I trade insight instead of labor or objects?
8. What would change if I saw perception as an asset to manage?
9. How could I act as a bridge rather than a competitor?
10. What small step could I take to become more trusted this quarter?

## Closing Reflection

Bartering brilliance is not about desperation. It is about **precision**.

When resources become unstable, the world does not reward hoarding—it rewards **alignment**. The people who thrive are not those with the most goods, but those who can make fragmented systems function again.

You do not need warehouses.
You do not need stockpiles.
You do not need permission.

You need **positioning**.

When you trade outcomes instead of objects, your value becomes lighter, faster, and harder to shut down.

You are no longer a consumer negotiating scarcity.

You are a connector engineering flow.

And in a post-water world, flow is wealth.

# Chapter 3: Water-Free Passive Income Systems

## Why Supply Chains Are the First Chokepoint

When scarcity intensifies, supply chains do not fail politely.

They fracture suddenly.

Roads close. Borders tighten. Fuel prices spike. Utilities fluctuate. Paperwork delays turn into shutdowns. Any income tied to **movement of matter** inherits every one of those risks.

Post-water wealth avoids the chokepoint entirely.

This chapter is not about side hustles or digital optimism. It is an **engineering manual** for income that persists when trucks stop moving and shelves stop refilling. Water-free income is not about ignoring reality—it is about designing around the most fragile dependency in modern economics: logistics.

If your income needs transportation, storage, or physical delivery, it is borrowing time.

This chapter teaches you how to stop borrowing.

## Passive Does Not Mean Lazy — It Means Decoupled

"Passive income" is often misunderstood.

In post-water economics, passive does not mean effortless. It means **decoupled**:

- Decoupled from location
- Decoupled from utilities
- Decoupled from daily presence
- Decoupled from physical throughput

Water-free systems are built once, refined, and then allowed to **operate independently of conditions**.

Your effort shifts from execution to **architecture**.

**The Zero-Inventory Advantage**

Inventory is invisible debt.
It must be:

- Stored
- Protected
- Insured
- Transported
- Liquidated

Under stress, inventory becomes exposure.
Water-free systems remove inventory entirely. You sell:

- Access
- Rights
- Knowledge
- Outcomes
- Permission

When nothing physical changes hands, nothing can be confiscated, delayed, spoiled, or stranded.

This is why zero-inventory models dominate resilient economies.

**Digital Assets as Income Engines**

Digital assets are not trends—they are **infrastructure replacements**.

Examples include:

- Educational content
- Frameworks and systems
- Templates and tools
- Databases
- Guides and playbooks

Once created, digital assets:

- Replicate infinitely
- Deliver instantly
- Survive border closures
- Scale without additional cost

The asset does not care about fuel prices, weather, or water access. It only requires **distribution**, which can be diversified.

**Licensing: Getting Paid Without Repeating Yourself**

Licensing is leverage in its purest form.

You create once.
Others deploy repeatedly.
You collect ongoing value.

Licensing converts:

- Knowledge into usage rights
- Systems into repeatable frameworks
- Ideas into income streams

Licenses survive chaos because they move **legally and conceptually**, not physically. They can be renegotiated, expanded, and localized without transport or inventory.

This is wealth that **travels without you**.

**Royalties: The Calmest Income Under Chaos**

Royalties are resilient because they are **downstream**.

You are paid after the system runs.

Books, audio, digital media, intellectual frameworks—these generate royalties because value is embedded once and distributed endlessly.

When panic rises, people seek:

- Guidance
- Explanation
- Structure
- Meaning

Royalties often **increase during instability** because demand for clarity spikes while physical consumption stalls.

This is income that remains calm while markets panic.

**Automation as Shock Absorption**

Automation is not about speed. It is about **continuity**.

Automated systems:

- Deliver without supervision
- Process transactions without delay
- Operate across time zones
- Continue during disruptions

When infrastructure strains, automated income does not stop working—it becomes more valuable because it **keeps working**.

You are not automating tasks. You are automating **reliability**.

### Platform-Agnostic Design

Platforms are convenient—and fragile.
If your income relies on:

- One website
- One payment processor
- One country
- One company's rules

It is exposed.
Water-free systems are platform-agnostic:

- Multiple distribution channels
- Redundant payment paths
- Transferable formats
- Portable audiences

You are not loyal to platforms.
Platforms are tools.

This design allows income to **reroute** under pressure rather than collapse.

**Asymmetric Micro-Services**
Micro-services do not sell time. They sell **precision**.
Examples include:

- Analysis
- Evaluation
- Planning
- Verification
- Strategic input

These services:

- Require minimal energy
- Deliver high value
- Do not scale workload linearly
- Travel digitally

A single insight can be worth more than hours of labor. This asymmetry allows income to persist even when personal capacity fluctuates.

**Decentralized Monetization**

Centralized systems fail loudly.
Decentralized systems fail quietly—or not at all.
Decentralized monetization includes:

- Multiple income sources
- Diverse audiences
- Distributed hosting
- Redundant delivery

When one node fails, others continue.
This is not paranoia. It is **engineering for resilience**.

### IP-Based Wealth: The Endgame

Intellectual property is the most water-free asset class available.

IP:

- Does not spoil
- Does not weigh anything
- Cannot be blockaded
- Scales globally

When infrastructure fails, IP becomes more valuable because it replaces broken systems with **understanding**.

This is why IP-based wealth dominates post-water economics. It survives environmental, political, and infrastructural stress simultaneously.

**Calm Income in Chaotic Times**

While others scramble for supplies, resilient systems continue to pay.
This creates psychological advantage.
When income is stable:

- Decisions improve
- Fear decreases
- Opportunities become visible

Those who panic pay premiums.
Those with calm income **collect positioning**.

### Journal Prompts

1. Which parts of my income depend on physical movement or inventory?
2. What knowledge do I already possess that could be turned into a digital asset?
3. Where am I repeating effort that could be systematized or licensed?
4. What would income look like if I removed location from the equation?
5. How exposed am I to a single platform or payment system?
6. What small automated system could I build this quarter?
7. Where could royalties replace one-time transactions?
8. What micro-service could I offer that delivers high value with low effort?
9. How could I decentralize my income streams to reduce risk?
10. What would "getting paid regardless" realistically look like for me?

### Closing Reflection

Water-free passive income is not about escaping work.

It is about escaping **fragility**.

When your income no longer depends on trucks, roads, utilities, or uninterrupted calm, your mind changes. You stop reacting to disruption and start **pricing it**.

You no longer ask how to secure supplies.

You ask how to secure **flow**.

And flow, once decoupled from physical constraints, becomes the most resilient form of wealth available.

From here on, you are no longer building income that moves through the world.

You are building income that **moves despite it**.

# Chapter 4: Investing in the Collapse

## Collapse Is Not Random — It Is Directional

Most people imagine collapse as a single moment: a sudden break, a dramatic end. In reality, collapse unfolds in **waves**. Systems weaken unevenly. Some sectors freeze while others overheat. Some assets implode while others quietly become indispensable.

This chapter teaches you to stop reacting emotionally to collapse and start **reading it as a market condition**.

Collapse is not the absence of opportunity. It is the **rearrangement of value under stress**.

Those who understand post-water economics do not ask, "Is this bad?"

They ask, **"Who benefits, who exits, and what is being mispriced right now?"**

**Why Panic Destroys Value**

Panic compresses time.

When people panic, they:

- Sell too early
- Sell too cheaply
- Abandon viable assets
- Accept unfavorable terms

This creates **desperation pricing**—assets exchanged for speed instead of value.

Collapse rewards those who can:

- Slow down decision-making
- Hold optionality
- Wait while others rush

The greatest financial advantage during collapse is not capital—it is **emotional control**.

**Mispriced Assets: The Signature of Collapse**

Every collapse creates mispricing.

Assets are not suddenly worthless—they are **misunderstood**.

Mispricing occurs when:

- Fear overrides analysis
- Liquidity disappears temporarily
- Narratives outrun reality
- Attention fixates on visible losses

Post-water investing focuses on identifying:

- Assets abandoned due to inconvenience, not failure
- Skills undervalued because they are not visible
- Systems misjudged because they operate quietly

You are not buying collapse.

You are buying **misinterpretation**.

**Fear-Driven Exits and the Opportunity They Leave Behind**
Fear does not just lower prices—it **empties rooms**.
When institutions wobble, people exit entire categories:

- Markets
- Careers
- Regions
- Skill domains

These exits leave behind:

- Undervalued positions
- Reduced competition
- Lower barriers to entry

Post-water investors understand that **crowds create scarcity of attention**. When attention collapses, opportunity expands.

**Forced Sellers: The Silent Engine of Opportunity**

Not all sellers choose to sell.

Collapse produces:

- Liquidity shortages
- Policy pressure
- Compliance deadlines
- Personal emergencies

Forced sellers accept unfavorable terms because they must.

This is not exploitation—it is **structural reality**. Prepared actors are positioned to absorb assets, roles, or access at prices that would never exist in calm conditions.

Those with water-free income can wait.

Those without it must sell.

**Attention Blindness During Chaos**
During collapse, attention narrows.
People focus on:

- Headlines
- Immediate threats
- Visible pain

They ignore:

- Secondary effects
- Long-term positioning
- Quiet infrastructure shifts

This blindness creates opportunity in:

- Support systems
- Coordination roles
- Transitional services
- Interpretation layers

The best investments during collapse are often invisible to those panicking.

**Investing in Resilience, Not Recovery**
Traditional investing looks for rebound.
Post-water investing looks for **resilience**.
Resilient assets:

- Function under constraint
- Adapt to multiple conditions
- Reduce dependence on single systems

Examples include:

- Coordination platforms
- Knowledge infrastructure
- Distributed services
- IP-based systems

You are not betting on normal returning.
You are betting on **function continuing**.

**Bottlenecks Are Where Value Accumulates**

Collapse creates bottlenecks.
Where systems slow, value condenses.
Bottlenecks include:

- Access points
- Decision authorities
- Compliance gateways
- Translation layers

Investing in bottlenecks means positioning yourself:

- Where flow must pass
- Where permission is required
- Where confusion concentrates

Those who control or alleviate bottlenecks extract disproportionate value during instability.

**Emotional Control as Financial Leverage**
Emotional regulation is an **investment skill**.
When others panic:

- You negotiate better
- You wait longer
- You choose strategically

Calm thinking compounds because it allows:

- Better timing
- Fewer mistakes
- Clearer pattern recognition

Desperation pays premiums.
Calm collects discounts.

**Preparation Beats Optimism**

Optimism assumes systems recover.
Preparation assumes **conditions persist**.
Post-water investors do not rely on hope. They rely on:

- Liquidity
- Flexibility
- Positioning
- Redundancy

Collapse rewards those who prepared quietly long before it was fashionable.

**Pricing Collapse Instead of Fearing It**

By now, collapse stops feeling abstract.
It becomes **measurable**.
You begin to ask:

- What is being abandoned prematurely?
- Who is selling because they must?
- Where has attention disappeared?
- What still functions despite stress?

This is not cynicism.
This is **strategic clarity**.

### Journal Prompts

1. How do I typically react emotionally when systems feel unstable?
2. Where have I seen panic cause people to make poor financial decisions?
3. What assets or roles are currently being abandoned due to fear?
4. Where might value be mispriced because of attention blindness?
5. What forms of resilience do I undervalue because they are quiet?
6. How could water-free income improve my ability to wait and choose?
7. What bottlenecks exist in my environment right now?
8. Where could calm positioning give me leverage?
9. What would preparation look like instead of optimism?
10. How can I start pricing collapse rather than fearing it?

### Closing Reflection

Collapse does not reward bravery.

It rewards **clarity**.

Those who thrive during instability are not reckless. They are not hopeful. They are prepared, patient, and emotionally regulated. They understand that panic is a cost, and calm is capital.

When others rush for exits, you watch where they leave doors open.

When others sell to survive, you buy to position.

You are no longer reacting to collapse.

You are **investing inside it**.

And once you learn to price instability, it loses its power to scare you.

## Chapter 5: Becoming a Hydration Lord

### The End of Asking for Security

Every previous chapter dismantled an external dependency.

This chapter dismantles the final one: **the belief that security comes from systems outside you**.

"Hydration Lord" is not a fantasy title. It is a functional identity—a person whose survival, income, and leverage do not collapse when conditions change. Not because they control resources, but because they **control response**.

Where dependency economics trains people to ask:

- *Who will provide?*
- *What happens if this stops?*
- *Who do I rely on now?*

Adaptive sovereignty replaces those questions with:

- *What options do I have?*
- *How fast can I reconfigure?*
- *Who relies on me?*

This chapter completes the transformation from participant to **infrastructure**.

**Why Hoarding Is the Lowest Form of Power**

In scarcity, the instinct to hoard feels logical.

It is also fragile.

Hoarding:

- Anchors you to place
- Increases visibility and risk
- Requires defense and secrecy
- Collapses once resources deplete

True power does not come from stockpiles. It comes from **positioning**.

A Hydration Lord does not hoard water. They ensure **flow**—of income, access, information, and coordination. When flow exists, resources follow. When hoarding exists, fear follows.

This is the final separation between desperation economics and sovereign economics.

**Sovereignty Is Optionality, Not Isolation**

Isolation is brittle.

Optionality is resilient.

Sovereignty does not mean cutting ties or becoming self-sufficient in every way. That is another form of dependency—this time on your own capacity.

Adaptive sovereignty means:

- Multiple income vectors
- Multiple roles you can occupy
- Multiple ways to exchange value
- Multiple exits and entries

You are sovereign when **no single failure can collapse you**.

The Hydration Lord is not alone. They are **connected on their terms.**

**Power Is Adaptability, Not Control**

Control requires stability.

Adaptability thrives in instability.

Those who seek control during collapse tighten rules, hoard authority, and overextend. Those who adapt redesign themselves faster than conditions change.

Adaptability includes:

- Learning faster than others panic
- Repositioning without identity loss
- Letting go of outdated roles
- Occupying emerging bottlenecks

The Hydration Lord does not dominate systems. They **outgrow them**.

**Wealth as Freedom of Response**

Traditional wealth is measured in accumulation.

Post-water wealth is measured in **response time**.

You are wealthy when:

- You can wait while others rush
- You can move while others freeze
- You can say no without consequence
- You can change strategy without collapse

Freedom of response is the highest form of wealth because it survives:

- Environmental stress
- Political instability
- Infrastructural failure
- Market panic

This is why income without supply chains matters. This is why perception matters. This is why calm thinking compounds.

Everything converges here.

**Integration of the Five Principles**

At this stage, the principles are no longer separate tools. They are **one operating system**.

- **Income without supply chains** keeps you solvent regardless of conditions
- **Knowledge and perception as currency** keeps you valuable without possession
- **Stress-proof wealth** keeps you operational under pressure
- **Anti-panic dominance** keeps your decisions clean
- **Self-directed economic authority** keeps you free

A Hydration Lord does not rely on a single income, platform, employer, or institution. They rely on **their ability to reconfigure value**.

**Becoming the System Others Rely On**

The final shift is subtle—and permanent.
You stop asking:

- *How do I fit into this system?*

You start asking:

- *What function am I providing that others cannot replace?*

When you:

- Coordinate under stress
- Translate chaos into clarity
- Maintain calm while others fracture
- Keep income flowing while others scramble

People orbit you.
Not out of loyalty.
Out of necessity.
This is not dominance.
It is **structural relevance**.

You become the person others depend on because you reduce uncertainty. And uncertainty is the most expensive resource in a post-water world.

**The Hydration Lord's Quiet Authority**

Authority does not announce itself.

It emerges.

The Hydration Lord:

- Is difficult to remove
- Easy to work with
- Valuable across contexts
- Calm under pressure

They do not broadcast power. They **demonstrate continuity**.

Where others demand guarantees, they provide options.

Where others hoard, they enable flow.

Where others collapse inward, they expand outward.

**The End of Dependency Economics**

Dependency economics promises safety in exchange for compliance.

It fails when conditions change.

Adaptive sovereignty promises nothing—but delivers **continuity**.

You no longer need permission to survive.

You no longer need systems to validate you.

You no longer wait for stability to return.

You have become fluid.

### Journal Prompts

1. Where in my life am I still seeking security from external systems?
2. What would optionality look like instead of control?
3. How do I personally respond when plans fail unexpectedly?
4. In what ways could I become harder to replace?
5. Where am I still hoarding instead of positioning?
6. What roles do I already occupy that reduce uncertainty for others?
7. How would my decisions change if I trusted my adaptability?
8. What does freedom of response mean for me personally?
9. Who already relies on me more than I realize?
10. What identity am I ready to release to become more sovereign?

### Closing Reflection

Becoming a Hydration Lord is not about domination, wealth displays, or survival bravado.

It is about **remaining intact when conditions refuse to cooperate**.

You have learned how value moves under scarcity.
You have learned how income can exist without infrastructure.
You have learned how calm outperforms panic.
You have learned how positioning beats possession.

Now you understand the final truth:

Security is not given.
It is **generated**.

You no longer seek protection from systems.

You **become one**.

And systems, whether they admit it or not, always protect what they depend on.

## Appendix A: The Liquidless Ledger – Emergency Wealth Plans

### What the Liquidless Ledger Is

The Liquidless Ledger is not a budget.

It is not a balance sheet.

It is a **decision framework for wealth continuity when normal assumptions fail**.

Traditional financial planning assumes:

- Banks function
- Utilities operate
- Markets open on schedule
- Rules remain stable
- Liquidity is available on demand

The Liquidless Ledger assumes **none of that**.

Instead, it tracks what *still works* when systems strain, fragment, or freeze. It is designed to help you **retain economic agency without relying on physical supply chains, clean water access, or institutional goodwill**.

This appendix turns the philosophy of the book into **actionable emergency wealth plans**—plans that can be activated immediately when conditions shift.

## Part I: The Ledger Mindset

### Wealth Under Stress Is About Continuity, Not Growth

In emergencies, growth is optional. **Continuity is mandatory**. The Liquidless Ledger prioritizes:

- Cash-flow survival
- Decision clarity
- Optionality
- Low-friction value exchange

If an asset cannot:

- Be accessed
- Be converted
- Be leveraged
- Or be ignored safely

Then it is not an emergency asset.

### The Core Question of the Ledger

Every entry in the Liquidless Ledger answers one question:

**"Does this help me get paid, stay flexible, or reposition when systems fail?"**

If the answer is no, it does not belong in the ledger—no matter how impressive it looks during stable times.

**Part II: The Five Columns of the Liquidless Ledger**

Each emergency wealth plan is built from five columns. You can write these physically, digitally, or mentally—but they must be **explicit**.

**Column 1: Income That Moves Without Matter**

List all income streams that:

- Require no inventory
- Require no shipping
- Require no physical presence
- Require no uninterrupted utilities

Examples:

- Digital products
- Royalties
- Licensing
- Remote advisory
- Coordination roles
- Automated services

**Emergency Rule:**

If income requires trucks, warehouses, or clean water to function, it is **non-primary** during stress.

**Column 2: Convertible Skills**
These are skills that:

- Reduce uncertainty
- Create alignment
- Translate chaos into decisions
- Function across industries and conditions

Examples:

- Strategy
- Organization
- Planning
- Interpretation
- Verification
- Teaching
- Coordination

**Emergency Rule:**
Skills that depend on a single environment are fragile. Skills that travel are sovereign.

**Column 3: Access & Position**
This column tracks **who you can reach and how quickly**.
Include:

- People you can coordinate
- Gateways you understand
- Informal channels
- Decision-makers
- Distribution paths

This is not networking.
This is **path awareness**.

**Emergency Rule:**
Access beats ownership when systems fragment.

**Column 4: Perception Capital**
Perception determines how fast value converts under stress.
List:

- What people trust you for
- What problems they associate you with solving
- Where your calm is visible
- Where your reliability has been proven

**Emergency Rule:**
Trust compresses negotiation. Distrust multiplies cost.

**Column 5: Optionality Reserves**

Optionality is not savings—it is **freedom of response**.

Optionality includes:

- Time
- Flexibility
- Low fixed expenses
- Multiple income paths
- Psychological readiness

**Emergency Rule:**

Optionality is more valuable than optimization when conditions shift.

**Part III: Emergency Wealth Scenarios**
The Liquidless Ledger is activated by **conditions**, not predictions. Below are core scenarios and how the ledger responds.

**Scenario 1: Utility Instability (Water, Power, Internet)**

**Ledger Response:**

- Shift income to lowest-bandwidth delivery
- Pause inventory-dependent activities
- Increase advisory, planning, and coordination roles
- Monetize clarity, not execution

**Wealth Focus:**
Getting paid for thinking, not producing.

**Scenario 2: Market Panic or Financial Freezes**

**Ledger Response:**

- Preserve calm income streams
- Avoid forced selling
- Increase perception-based services
- Identify panic-driven mispricing

**Wealth Focus:**
Waiting while others rush.

**Scenario 3: Border Closures or Regulatory Shifts**

**Ledger Response:**

- Use platform-agnostic distribution
- Redirect offerings digitally
- License rather than sell
- Decentralize monetization paths

**Wealth Focus:**
Rerouting, not resisting.

### Scenario 4: Personal Capacity Loss (Illness, Burnout, Crisis)

**Ledger Response:**

- Lean on automated systems
- Activate royalties and licenses
- Reduce effort-heavy services
- Maintain minimum viable income

**Wealth Focus:**
Survival without heroics.

**Scenario 5: Social or Institutional Breakdown**

**Ledger Response:**

- Occupy coordination roles
- Reduce visibility of physical assets
- Increase value through mediation and structure
- Become indispensable quietly

**Wealth Focus:**
Being the stabilizing function.

## Part IV: The Emergency Wealth Tiers

Use these tiers to assess your current position.

### Tier 1: Fragile

- Income tied to physical presence
- High dependency on utilities
- Single point of failure
- No automation
- Panic-prone decisions

**Action:**

Convert effort into abstraction immediately.

### Tier 2: Reactive

- Some digital income
- Limited redundancy
- Partial optionality
- Still dependent on stability

**Action:**
Reduce bottlenecks. Build buffers.

**Tier 3: Resilient**

- Multiple water-free income streams
- Transferable skills
- Calm under stress
- Some coordination power

**Action:**
Strengthen perception and access.

### Tier 4: Sovereign

- Income decoupled from infrastructure
- Recognized for clarity and coordination
- Optionality exceeds dependence
- Others rely on your function

**Action:**
Maintain invisibility. Protect flexibility.

**Part V: The Emergency Activation Checklist**

When conditions shift, run this checklist immediately:

- What income still functions **today**?
- What can be paused without harm?
- Where is panic creating mispricing?
- Who needs clarity right now?
- What role can I occupy that reduces uncertainty?
- What decision can I delay safely?
- What exposure can I quietly remove?

This checklist is not about speed.
It is about **precision**.

**Part VI: The Ledger as a Living System**

The Liquidless Ledger is not filled once.

It is **revised continuously**.

After every disruption, ask:

- What failed unexpectedly?
- What held?
- What gained value?
- What was harder to replace than expected?

Then update the ledger.

The Hydration Lord does not cling to outdated plans. They revise without sentiment.

**Closing Statement: Wealth Without Water, Revisited**

The Liquidless Ledger exists for one purpose:

**To ensure you are never forced into desperation thinking.**

When others scramble for supplies, you preserve flow.
When others sell under pressure, you wait.
When others freeze, you reposition.

This appendix completes the book's promise.

You no longer measure wealth by accumulation.

You measure it by **continuity, optionality, and response**.

And when water becomes unreliable, that is the only wealth that lasts.

**Message from the Author:**

I hope you enjoyed this book, I love astrology and knew there was not a book such as this out on the shelf. I love metaphysical items as well. Please check out my other books:

-Life of Government Benefits

-My life of Hell

-My life with Hydrocephalus

-Red Sky

-World Domination:Woman's rule

-World Domination:Woman's Rule 2: The War

-Life and Banishment of Apophis: book 1

-The Kidney Friendly Diet

-The Ultimate Hemp Cookbook

-Creating a Dispensary(legally)

-Cleanliness throughout life: the importance of showering from childhood to adulthood.

-Strong Roots: The Risks of Overcoddling children

-Hemp Horoscopes: Cosmic Insights and Earthly Healing

- Celestial Hemp Navigating the Zodiac: Through the Green Cosmos

-Astrological Hemp: Aligning The Stars with Earth's Ancient Herb

-The Astrological Guide to Hemp: Stars, Signs, and Sacred Leaves

-Green Growth: Innovative Marketing Strategies for your Hemp Products and Dispensary

-Cosmic Cannabis

-Astrological Munchies

-Henry The Hemp

-Zodiacal Roots: The Astrological Soul Of Hemp

- **Green Constellations: Intersection of Hemp and Zodiac**

-Hemp in The Houses: An astrological Adventure Through The Cannabis Galaxy

-Galactic Ganja Guide

Heavenly Hemp

Zodiac Leaves

Doctor Who Astrology

Cannastrology

Stellar Satvias and Cosmic Indicas

Celestial Cannabis: A Zodiac Journey

AstroHerbology: The Sky and The Soil: Volume 1

AstroHerbology:Celestial Cannabis:Volume 2

Cosmic Cannabis Cultivation

The Starry Guide to Herbal Harmony: Volume 1

The Starry Guide to Herbal Harmony: Cannabis Universe: Volume 2

Yugioh Astrology: Astrological Guide to Deck, Duels and more

Nightmare Mansion: Echoes of The Abyss

**Nightmare Mansion 2: Legacy of Shadows**

**Nightmare Mansion 3: Shadows of the Forgotten**

Nightmare Mansion 4: Echoes of the Damned

The Life and Banishment of Apophis: Book 2

Nightmare Mansion: Halls of Despair

Healing with Herb: Cannabis and Hydrocephalus

**Planetary Pot: Aligning with Astrological Herbs: Volume 1**

**Fast Track to Freedom: 30 Days to Financial Independence Using AI, Assets, and Agile Hustles**

**Cosmic Hemp Pathways**

**How to Become Financially Free in 30 Days: 10,000 Paths to Prosperity**

**Zodiacal Herbage: Astrological Insights: Volume 1**

Nightmare Mansion: Whispers in the Walls

The Daleks Invade Atlantis

**Henry the hemp and Hydrocephalus**

10X The Kidney Friendly Diet

Cannabis Universe: Adult coloring book

**Hemp Astrology: The Healing Power of the Stars**

**Zodiacal Herbage: Astrological Insights: Cannabis Universe: Volume 2**

**Planetary Pot: Aligning with Astrological Herbs: Cannabis Universes: Volume 2**

**Doctor Who: Convergence Protocol – The Replicator War**

Nightmare Mansion: Curse of the Blood Moon

**The Celestial Stoner: A Guide to the Zodiac**

**Cosmic Pleasures: Sex Toy Astrology for Every Sign**

Hydrocephalus Astrology: Navigating the Stars and Healing Waters

**Lapis and the Mischievous Chocolate Bar**

Celestial Positions: Sexual Astrology for Every Sign

Apophis's Shadow Work Journal: **:** A Journey of Self-Discovery and Healing

**Kinky Cosmos: Sexual Kink Astrology for Every Sign**

**Digital Cosmos: The Astrological Digimon Compendium**

**Stellar Seeds: The Cosmic Guide to Growing with Astrology**

Apophis's Daily Gratitude Journal

Cat Astrology: Feline Mysteries of the Cosmos

**The Cosmic Kama Sutra: An Astrological Guide to Sexual Positions**

**Unleash Your Potential: A Guided Journal Powered by AI Insights**

**Whispers of the Enchanted Grove**

Cosmic Pleasures: An Astrological Guide to Sexual Kinks

369, 12 Manifestation Journal

Whisper of the nocturne journal(blank journal for writing or drawing)

The Boogey Book

Locked In Reflection: A Chastity Journey Through Locktober

Generating Wealth Quickly:How to Generate $100,000 in 24 Hours

Star Magic: Harness the Power of the Universe

The Flatulence Chronicles: A Fart Journal for Self-Discovery

The Doctor and The Death Moth

Seize the Day: A Personal Seizure Tracking Journal

The Ultimate Boogeyman Safari: A Journey into the Boogie World and Beyond

**Whispers of Samhain: 1,000 Spells of Love, Luck, and Lunar Magic: Samhain Spell Book**

**Apophis's guides:Witch's Spellbook Crafting Guide for Halloween**

**Frost & Flame: The Enchanted Yule Grimoire of 1000 Winter Spells**

**The Ultimate Boogey Goo Guide & Spooky Activities for Halloween Fun**

Harmony of the Scales: A Libra's Spellcraft for Balance and Beauty

The Enchanted Advent: 36 Days of Christmas Wonders

Nightmare Mansion: The Labyrinth of Screams

Harvest of Enchantment: 1,000 Spells of Gratitude, Love, and Fortune for Thanksgiving

The Boogey Chronicles: A Journal of Nightly Encounters and Shadowy Secrets

The 12 Days of Financial Freedom: A Step-by-Step Christmas Countdown to Transform Your Finances

Sigil of the Eternal Spiral Blank Journal

A Christmas Feast: Timeless Recipes for Every Meal

Holiday Stress-Free Solutions: A Survival Guide to Thriving During the Festive Season

Yu-Gi-Oh! Holiday Gifting Mastery: The Ultimate Guide for Fans and Newcomers Alike

Holiday Harmony: A Hydrocephalus Survival Guide for the Festive Season

Celestial Craft: The Witch's Almanac for 2025 – A Cosmic Guide to Manifestations, Moons, and Mystical Events

Doctor Who: The Toymaker's Winter Wonderland

Tulsa King Unveiled: A Thrilling Guide to Stallone's Mafia Masterpiece

Pendulum Craft: A Complete Guide to Crafting and Using Personalized Divination Tools

Nightmare Mansion: Santa's Eternal Eve

Starlight Noel: A Cosmic Journey through Christmas Mysteries

The Dark Architect: Unlocking the Blueprint of Existence

Surviving the Embrace: The Ultimate Guide to Encounters with The Hugging Molly

The Enchanted Codex: Secrets of the Craft for Witches, Wiccans, and Pagans

Harvest of Gratitude: A Complete Thanksgiving Guide

Yuletide Essentials: A Complete Guide to an Authentic and Magical Christmas

Celestial Smokes: A Cosmic Guide to Cigars and Astrology

Living in Balance: A Comprehensive Survival Guide to Thriving with Diabetes Insipidus

Cosmic Symbiosis: The Venom Zodiac Chronicles

***The Cursed Paw of Ambition***

Cosmic Symbiosis: The Astrological Venom Journal

Celestial Wonders Unfold: A Stargazer's Guide to the Cosmos (2024-2029)

The Ultimate Black Friday Prepper's Guide: Mastering Shopping Strategies and Savings

*Cosmic Sales: The Astrological Guide to Black Friday Shopping*

Legends of the Corn Mother and Other Harvest Myths

Whispers of the Harvest: The Corn Mother's Journal

The Evergreen Spellbook

The Doctor Meets the Boogeyman

The White Witch of Rose Hall's SpellBook

**The Gingerbread Golem's Shadow: A Study in Sweet Darkness**

**The Gingerbread Golem Codex: An Academic Exploration of Sweet Myths**

The Gingerbread Golem Grimoire: Sweet Magicks and Spells for the Festive Witch

**The Curse of the Gingerbread Golem**

10-minute Christmas Crafts for kids

**Christmas Crisis Solutions: The Ultimate Last-Minute Survival Guide**

Gingerbread Golem Recipes: Holiday Treats with a Magical Twist

***The Infinite Key: Unlocking Mystical Secrets of the Ages***

Enchanted Yule: A Wiccan and Pagan Guide to a Magical and Memorable Season

Dinosaurs of Power: Unlocking Ancient Magick

Astro-Dinos: The Cosmic Guide to Prehistoric Wisdom

Gallifrey's Yule Logs: A Festive Doctor Who Cookbook

**The Dino Grimoire: Secrets of Prehistoric Magick**

**The Gift They Never Knew They Needed**

*The Gingerbread Golem's Culinary Alchemy: Enchanting Recipes for a Sweetly Dark Feast*

A Time Lord Christmas: Holiday Adventures with the Doctor

**Krampusproofing Your Home: Defensive Strategies for Yule**

Silent Frights: A Collection of Christmas Creepypastas to Chill Your Bones

***Santa Raptor's Jolly Carnage: A Dino-Claus Christmas Tale***

Prehistoric Palettes: A Dino Wicca Coloring Journey

The Christmas Wishkeeper Chronicles

The Starlight Sleigh: A Holiday Journey

***Elf Secrets: The True Magic of the North Pole***

Candy Cane Conjurations

***Cooking with Kids: Recipes Under 20 Minutes***

Doctor Who: The TARDIS Confiscation

*The Anxiety First Aid Kit: Quick Tools to Calm Your Mind*

Frosty Whispers: A Winter's Tale

The Infinite Key: Unlocking the Secrets to Prosperity, Resilience, and Purpose

The Grasping Void: Why You'll Regret This Purchase

Astrology for Busy Bees: Star Signs Simplified

***The Instant Focus Formula: Cut Through the Noise***

The Secret Language of Colors: Unlocking the Emotional Codes

Sacred Fossil Chronicles: Blank Journal

**The Christmas Cottage Miracle**

**Feeding Frenzy: Graboid-Inspired Recipes**

**Manifest in Minutes: The Quick Law of Attraction Guide**

**The Symbiote Chronicles: Doctor Who's Venomous Journey**

**Think Tiny, Grow Big: The Minimalist Mindset**

**The Energy Key: Unlocking Limitless Motivation**

New Year, New Magic: Manifesting Your Best Year Yet

Unstoppable You: Mastering Confidence in Minutes

Infinite Energy: The Secret to Never Feeling Drained

Lightning Focus: Mastering the Art of Productivity in a Distracted World

Saturnalia Manifestation Magick: A Guide to Unlocking Abundance During the Solstice

Graboids and Garland: The Ultimate Tremors-Themed Christmas Guide

12 Nights of Holiday Magic

The Power of Pause: 60-Second Mindfulness Practices

The Quick Reset: How to Reclaim Your Life After Burnout

The Shadow Eater: A Tale of Despair and Survival

The Micro-Mastery Method: Transform Your Skills in Just Minutes a Day

Reclaiming Time: How to Live More by Doing Less

Chronovore: The Eternal Nexus

The Mind Reset: Unlocking Your Inner Peace in a Chaotic World

Confidence Code: Building Unshakable Self-Belief

Baby the Vampire Terrier
Baby the Vampire Terrier's Christmas Adventure
Celestial Streams: The Content Creator's Astrology Manual
The Wealth Whisperer: Unlocking Abundance with Everyday Actions
The Energy Equation: Maximize Your Output Without Burning Out
The Happiness Algorithm: Science-Backed Steps to Joyful Living
Stress-Free Success: Achieving Goals Without Anxiety
Mindful Wealth: The New Blueprint for Financial Freedom
The Festive Flavors of New Year: A Culinary Celebration
The Master's Gambit: Keys of Eternal Power
Shadowed Secrets: Groundhog Day Mysteries
Beneath the Burrow: Lessons from the Groundhog
Spring's Whispers: The Groundhog's Prediction
The Limitless Mindset: Unlock Your Untapped Potential
The Focus Funnel: How to Cut Through Chaos and Get Results
Bold Moves: Building Courage to Live on Your Terms
The Daily Shift: Simple Practices for Lasting Transformation
The Quarter-Life Reset: Thriving in Your 20s and 30s
The Art of Shadowplay: Building Your Own Personal Myth
**The Eternal Loop: Finding Purpose in Repetition**
**Burrowing Wisdom: Life Lessons from the Groundhog**
**Shadow Work: A Groundhog Day Perspective**
**Love in Bloom: 5-Minute Romantic Gestures**
**The Shadowspell Codex: Secrets of Forbidden Magick**
**The Burnout Cure: Finding Balance in a Busy World**
**The Groundhog Prophecy: Unlocking Seasonal Secrets**
**Nog Tales: The Spirited History of Eggnog**
**Six More Weeks: Embracing Seasonal Transitions**
**The Lumivian Chronicles: Fragments of the Fifth Dimension**
**Money on Your Mind: A Beginner's Guide to Wealth**
**The Focus Fix: Breaking Through Distraction**

**January's Spirit Keepers: Mystical Protectors of the Cold**
**Creativity Unchained: Unlocking Your Wildest Ideas in 2025**
**Manifestation Mastery: 365 Days to Rewrite Your Reality**
**The Groundhog's Mirror: Reflecting on Change**
**The Weeping Angels' Christmas Curse**
**Burrowed in Time: A Groundhog Day Journey**
**Heartbeats: Poems to Share with Your Valentine**
**Dino Wicca: The Sacred Grimoire of Prehistoric Magick**
**Courage of the Pride: Finding Your Inner Roar**
**The Lion's Leap: Bold Moves for Big Results**
**Healthy Hustle: Achieving Without Overworking**
**Practical Manifesting: Turning Dreams into Reality in 2025**
**Jurassic Pharaohs: Unlocking the Magick of Ancient Egypt and Dino Wicca**
**The Happiness Equation: Small Changes for Big Joy**
**The Confidence Compass: Finding Your Inner Strength**
**Whispers in the Hollow: Tales of the Forgotten Beasts**
**Echoes from the Hollow: The Return of Forgotten Beasts**
**The Hollow Ascendant: The Rise of the Forgotten Beasts**
**The Relationship Reset: Building Better Connections**
**Mastering the Morning: How to Win the Day Before 8 AM**
**The Shadow's Dance: Groundhog Day Symbolism**
**Cupid's Kitchen: Quick Valentine's Day Recipes**
**Valentine's Day on a Budget: Love Without Breaking the Bank**
**Astrocraft: Aligning the Stars in the World of Minecraft**
**Forecasting Life: Groundhog Day Reflections**

Bleeding Hearts: Twisted Tales of Valentine's Terror

Herbal Smoke Revolution: The Ultimate Guide to Nature's Cigarette Alternative

Winter's Wrath: The Complete Survival Blueprint for Extreme Freezes.

**The Groundhog's Shadow: A Tale of Seasons**
**Burrowed Insights: Wisdom from the Groundhog**

**Sensual Strings: The Art of Erotic Bondage**
**Whispered Flames: Unlocking the Power of Fire Play**
**Forgotten Shadows: A Guide to Cryptids Lost to Time**
**Six Weeks of Secrets: Groundhog Day's Hidden Messages**
**Shadows and Cycles: Groundhog Day Reflections**
**The Art of Love Letters: Crafting the Perfect Message**
**Romantic Getaways at Home: Turning Your Space into Paradise**
**Purrfect Brews: A Cat Lover's Guide to Coffee and Companionship**
**The Groundhog's Wisdom: Timeless Lessons for Modern Life**
**The Shadow Oracle: Groundhog Day as a Predictor**
**Emerging from the Burrow: A Journey of Renewal**
**The Language of Love: Learning Your Partner's Love Style**
**Authorpreneur: The Ultimate Blueprint for Writing, Publishing, and Thriving as an Author**
**Weathering the Seasons: Groundhog Day Perspectives**
**Valentine's Day Magic: A Guide to Romantic Rituals**
**The Shadow Chronicles: Stories of Groundhog Day**
**Love and Laughter: Fun Games for Valentine's Day**
**AstroRealty: Unlocking the Stars for Property Success**
**The Groundhog's Path: A Guide to Seasonal Balance**
**Groundhog Day Diaries: Reflections in the Shadow**
**The Groundhog's Light: Illuminating the Path Ahead**
**Valentine's Traditions from Around the World**
**AI Wealth Revolution: Unlocking the Trillionaire Mindset**
**Love Rekindled: Reigniting Passion in Relationships**
**Single and Thriving: Self-Love on Valentine's Day**
**Emerald Legends: Mystical Tales of Ireland**
**Green Alchemy: Harnessing Nature's Magic**
**The Hearts of Horror: A Valentine's Day Nightmare**
**The Leprechaun's Guide to Wealth and Wisdom**
**Dancing with the Sidhe: Celebrating the Otherworld**

**Shamrocks and Shadows: Mysteries of the Green Isle**

**Emerald Energy: Harnessing Luck and Growth**

**The Gingerbread Golem's Valentine: A Sweetheart's Guide to Love and Enchantment**

**The Celtic Knot: Weaving Life and Destiny**

**Green Fire: Elemental Magic for St. Patrick's Day**

**Clover Chronicles: Finding Your Inner Luck**

**Ireland's Mystical Creatures: A Field Guide**

**Gingerbread Golem's Love Almanac**

**Prowl and Thrive: The Lion's Guide to Success**

**Love Alchemy: Transforming Your Life Through Heart Energy**

WORLD DOMINATION: Woman's Rule 3:The New Life

**The Midnight Rose: A Guide to Lunar Love Spells**

**The Forbidden Letters: Writing Your Own Love Prophecy**

**Luck and Lore: St. Patrick's Day for Modern Mystics**

**The Green Path: A Pagan Celebration of Renewal**

**The Dark Architect's Guide to Reprogramming Reality**

**Prankster's Paradise: A Guide to Harmless Hijinks**

**Manifest Your Reality: The Law of Attraction Simplified**

**The TARDIS Owner's Manual: Understanding the Doctor's Ship:** *A complete guide to the TARDIS, its technology, secrets, and mysteries*

**Starlit Romance: Astrology Secrets for Finding True Love**

**The Time Lord's Atlas: A Complete Guide to the Whoniverse:** ***A breakdown of the locations, planets, and dimensions explored in Doctor Who***

**Sweetheart Shadows: The Dark Side of Love and Attraction**

**February Fire: Reigniting Passion in Every Area of Life**

**The Self-Love Toolkit: 5 Ways to Embrace Who You Are**

***February Sparks: Ignite Your Dreams in 28 Days***

**March to Success: A 31-Day Action Blueprint**

**Ancient Paths: The 13 Sacred Principles of Dino Wicca**

**Echoes of Tomorrow: Navigating the AI Revolution**
**The Wellness Blueprint: Balancing Mind, Body, and Soul**
**Green Horizons: Sustainable Living for a Better Tomorrow**
**The AI Wealth Code: How to Make Millions with Automation**
**AI-Powered Creativity: Writing, Art, and Music for Profit**
**Extinction Rites: Rebirthing Your Soul Through Prehistoric Magick**
**Sacred Serpents tarot**
**Celestial Enchantment blank journal**
**Star Strains**
**Culinary Journeys: Exploring Global Flavors at Home**
**The Hollowvale Curse**
**The Hollowvale Harvest**
**The Egg of Transformation: Awakening Your Inner Power**
**Blooming Into Power: A Wiccan Guide to Spring Awakening**
**The Nightmare Nexus: The Third Doctor's Perilous Haunting**
**Digital Detox: Reclaiming Your Life in a Connected World**
**Ostara's Path: Walking the Spiral of Renewal**
**The Sacred Hare**
**Financial Freedom: Building Wealth in the Modern Age**
**Spring's Cauldron: Stirring the Waters of Change**
**The Hollowvale Pact**
**Quantum Consciousness: The Science of Reality Shifting**
**The Hollowvale Hunger**
**The Sacred Waters Within: A Witch's Guide to Hydrocephalus Magick**
**The Raven's Nest: Building a Life of Unshakable Stability**
**AI and the Human Mind: The Future of Intelligence**
**The Hollowvale Reckoning**
**Timeless Love: Building and Maintaining Lasting Relationships**
**The Raven's Roar: Unlocking Unstoppable Confidence**
**Raven Sight: Awakening Intuition and Inner Wisdom**

**The Butterfly Effect: Small Changes, Big Transformations**

**Taming the Boogeyman: How to Conquer Your Inner Fears**

**The Magick of Green: Awakening Earth's Energy in You**

The Entrepreneurial Mindset: Secrets to Business Success

**The Hollowvale End**

**The Shadow Luck Ritual: Reclaiming Power from Your Dark Side**

**Spring Magick for Beginners: A Simple Guide to Seasonal Energy Work**

**Doctor Who: The Hollowvale Conundrum**

**The March of Miracles: Unlocking Synchronicities in Spring**

**Unveiling the Cosmos: A Guide to Stargazing and Space Exploration**

**The Ultimate Guide to Surviving an Economic Collapse**

**The AI Gold Rush: How to Profit from the AI Revolution**

**Bastet's Shadow: The Hidden Power of Feline Magick**

**The Bastet Codex: Unlocking the Goddess's Magickal Secrets**

**Purring Spells: Harnessing Bastet's Healing Frequencies**

**Bastet's Nine Lives: Rebirth, Transformation, and Immortality Spells**

**Primal Currents: Hydrocephalus Magick in the Path of Dino Wicca**

**The Digital Gold Rush: Mastering E-Commerce and Online Sales**

**Future Shock: Adapting to the Next Decade of Change**

**The Quantum Mindset: Think Like a Billionaire**

**Sacred Motherhood: Awakening the Divine Feminine Within**

**The Mother's Spellbook: Enchantments for Love, Protection, and Prosperity**

**The Witch's Guide to Parenting: Raising Empowered and Intuitive Children**

**The Magick of Motherhood: Reclaiming Your Power Through Rituals**

**The Pagan Path to Self-Love: A Goddess's Guide to Worth and Confidence**
**Wild Woman Magick: Unleashing Your Primal Power**
**The Money Magnet Blueprint: Unlocking Unlimited Wealth**
**Biohacking 101: Unlock Your Body's Full Potential**
**The Wild Father: A Pagan Guide to Strength and Wisdom**
**The Sacred Masculine: Unlocking Your Inner Power**
**The Druid's Compass**
**The Warrior's Mindset**
**The Father's Fire**
**Odin's Path**
**Ancestral Bonds**
**The House That Whispers**
**The Magician's Code**
**The Wild Hunt**
**The Green Man's Path**
**The Altar of Success**
**The Shadow and the Sword**
**The High Priestess's Guide to Energy Healing**
**The Lunar Mother**
**The Sacred Self-Care Grimoire**
**The Womb Wisdom Codex**
**The Wheel of the Mother**
**The Witch's Guide to Manifestation**
**The Q2 Reset**
**The Ultimate Guide to AI-Powered Passive Income**
**Escape the 9-5**
**AI Feline Fortunes**
**The Tear-Stained Grimoire**
**Razorblade Runes**
**Cemetery Sirens**
**The Midnight Wristwatch**
**The Town That Forgets**

**AI Horror & Creepypasta**
**The Hollow Frequency**
**The Breach Echo**
**The Quiet Between Worlds**
**The Sigil of Tharan-Khul**
**Summon the Vault of Y'ha'ten**
**The Becoming Codex**
**The Profit of Az'ra-nar**
**The Drowned Logos**
**Echoes of the Eldritch Will**
**The Deep Ledger**
**Necronomicon of Networth**
**Covenant of the Wealthwyrm**
**The Whisperer's Manifesto**
**The Rites of Azh-K'luth**
**The Ark of the Crawling Coin**
**The Tithe of Shadows**
**Inkheart Abyss**
**The Timewinds of Y'ha-nthlei**
**The Spiral Labyrinth of Azag-Nirrh**
**The Gallifreyan Heresy of the Black Pharaoh**
**The Psalms of Nyog-Sotha**
**Black Rain Alchemy**
**The Infinite Maw**
**The Entropic Blueprint**
**The Oracle of Sh'guul**
**The Book of Breach**
**The Drowned Saint's Testament**
**Dreamcraft of the Sleeper God**
**The Silence Market**
**Cthonomics: The Dark Wealth Algorithm**
**Invocation of the Ten-Eyed King**
**Wealthbound to the Wyrm Below**

**Become the Unnameable**
**Codex of the Sovereign Flame**
**Rituals of Relentless Becoming**
**The Shadow Ascends**
**The Eyes Beneath You**
**The Will That Wakes Worlds**
**Silence Is a Weapon**
**The Mirror That Screams**
**The Whisper Between Moments**
**The Mind That Devours Fear**
**The Myth of the Finished Self**
**The Architect of Your Madness**
**The Voice You've Buried**
**The Discipline of Madness**
**Stormborn: Awakening Your Inner Tempest**
**The Mind That Ate Time**
**Unbind Your Becoming**
**The Pact You Owe Yourself**
**The Devourer's Diet**
**The Acid That Carves the Path**
**The Tower You Must Burn**
**The Breath Between Worlds**
**Speak Like the Deep**
**The Labyrinth Within**
**The Spine of the Sea God**
**Rejection Is a Portal**
**The Crown You Refused**
**The Scar Is the Spell**
**The Lightless Flame**
**The Habit of Becoming Horrific**
**ChickenJockey Chaos**
**The Gatekeeper Within**
**You Are Not Your Name**

**The Compass of the Mad**
**The Archive of Unsent Letters**
**What the Mirror Can't Show You**
**The Knife You Needed**
**Worship Nothing, Become Everything**
**The Other Voice**
**The Body the World Forgot**
**The Vein of the Void**
**The Black Bone Codex**
**The Puzzle of the Hidden Self (Millennium Puzzle)**
**The Eye That Sees the Lie** *(Millennium Eye)*
**The Ring of Return (Millennium Ring)**
**The Rod of Relentless Will *(Millennium Rod)***
**The Tally of the Soul (Millennium Tauk/Necklace)**
**The Key to the Locked Timeline (Millennium Key)**
**The Scale of Sacred Decisions (Millennium Scales)**
**Inferno Bites: The UnOfficial Minecraft Lava Cookbook**
**Rot in the Attic**
**Prana: The Hidden Force of Your Infinite Self**
**The Shadow Realm Within: Transforming Darkness Into Destiny**
**The Borderland Collapse**
**Claws of Protection: Bastet's Defensive Magick**
**Mr. Ring-a-Ding's Madness**
**Yugioh Astrology: Celestial Deckcraft and Duel Destiny (2026–2027 Edition)**
**The Seal You Signed: Unlocking the Power You Once Feared**
**The Puzzle of Infinite Minds: Unlocking the Mentalism Hidden Within**
**The Eye That Mirrors the All: Secrets of Inner Reflection**
**Doctor Who: The Toymaker's Broadcast**
**The Rod of Eternal Flow: Commanding the Currents of Vibration**

**Doctor Who: The World That Froths**
**Rootwake: The Fizz That Rewrites Flesh**
**Rootwake: Frothfather of the World**
**The Holly Pact: Blood Beneath the Mistletoe**
**The 2nd Mass Principle: Building Unbreakable Tribes**
**Web of Wits: A Survival Guide to Encounters with Anasi the Spider (Aunt Nancy)**
**The Hexbreaking Handbook: Effective Spells to Remove Curses**
**Pop Alchemy: Transform Your Life One Sip at a Time**
**The Mason Code: Leading in Unleadable Times**
**Petosiris and the Fifth Chamber of Thoth**
**The Ether Seed Within**
**The Parent of Tomorrow**
**Petosiris's Pyramid of Perpetual Wealth**
**Unlearn the World**
**Grimoire of the Hollow Tongue**
**Zodiac Weeds: Finding Your Strain Through the Stars**
**Aquarius Rises in the Bank**
**The Sugar God's Smile**
**The Skinclock Reversal: Biohacking the Face of Time**
**Debtburn: How to Obliterate What You Owe Forever**
**The Ice Cream Oracle: What Your Cone Says About Your Future**
**Silence Is Sovereignty: The Power of Being Unreadable**
**The Wind That Whispers Through Stone**
**Path of the Four Directions**
**Doctor Who: The Maestro's Symphony of Endings**
**Oxygen Grail: Breathing to Undo the Clock**
**Zodiacal Collapse: When Stars Devour Time**
**Teachings from the Red Sand Silence**
**Doctor Who: Omega – The Broken Equation**
**Memory Wipe Your Past: Start Over Like a MiB**

**Mitochondria Prime: Ignite the Core of Youth**

**A Nest of Roaches**

**Grub from the Galaxy: MiB Recipes You'll Never Forget**

**Whiskers of Power: Bastet's Guide to Inner Sovereignty**

**The Gift Must Cost Them: Negotiation Through Unequal Exchange**

**The Worm Guys' Wealth Code: Hustle Like an Alien**

**Bug Out: The Edgar Method for Ruthless Goal Setting**

**Weaving Life with Spiderwoman's Pattern**

**Doctor Who: The Rani's Renaissance**

**How to Get a Job (If You're a Puppygirl)**

**Speak Through Others: The Art of Proxy Power**

**T-Rex Your Trauma: Reclaim the Power of Your Primal Self**

**The Black Briefcase: How MiB Stay Wealthy in Silence**

**The Thirst Beyond Reason: Understanding Diabetes Insipidus From the Inside Out**

**Backwoods Witchcraft for Billionaires: The Pagan Path from Dirt Roads to Gold Roads**

**The Moonshine Grimoire: Fermented Spells for Abundance**

*The Nameless Geometry*

*The Wraith's Mixtape: Spellcasting with Songs of Sorrow*

**The Gallifreyan Gentleman: Silent Wealth, Sonic Confidence, and the Doctor's Code of Living**

*Sugar Water Confidence*

*Dino Totems: Spirit Guides from Earth's First Gods*

*Pumpkin Sigils & Ritual Smoke*

**The Hózhó Compass**

**The Distortus Discipline – Order from Inner Mutation**

**Witchcraft for the Cold-Blooded Soul**

**Moonlight Over the Blessingway**

**Water, Interrupted: When the Body Forgets How to Hold On**

**Deformed but Divine: Embracing Your Asymmetry**

**Hexes in the Henhouse: The Farm Witch's Guide to Power**

**The Reversed Flame: A Grimoire of Inverted Power**

*Salt, Cells, and Sanity: Reclaiming Balance with Diabetes Insipidus*

**King of the Broken: Crowning the Flawed Self**

**Moonlight Scars: Emo Moon Magick and the Art of Lunar Sorrow**

**Noose Spells: Magick of the Hanging Rope**

**The Goth Cathedral: Rituals of the Broken and Beautiful**

**The Cretaceous Codex: Dino Spirits and Fossil Magick**

**The Turkey Bones Ritual**

**Nine Lives of Manifestation: Unlocking Bastet's Reality Codes**

**Chaos Muscles: Building Strength from Twisted Pain**

**Emo Blood Magick: The Veins of Power**

**The 3AM Flood: Nighttime Urination, Sleep Loss, and the DI Spiral**

**The Silence Between the Stars**

**The Lemon Method: Sour Your Way to Success**

**Starlit Sovereign**

*The Rite of Twelve Gates: Walking the Gates of the Duat.*

**Cornbread and Conjure: Recipes for Riches and Rootwork**

**The Black Rose Rituals: Emo Love Spells and Obsession Magick**

**The Eternal Goodbye: Death Magick and Rebirth Rituals**

**Sinkrot: The Drain That Remembers**

**The Hybrid Mindset: Thinking Beyond Evolution**

*Bone Dry: Navigating Dehydration Before It Breaks You*

**Wreathcraft: Winter Sigils and Yuletide Spells**

**The Rite of Twelve Mouths**

**S'mores of the Damned: Haunted Recipes for Halloween Night**

**Rethink the Drink: A Beverage Survival Guide for DI Warriors**

**The Shadow Chord: Guitar Magick and Sonic**

**Malformed Yet Majestic: Leading When You Feel Wrong Inside**
**The Cursed Diary: Ink-Stained Spells of the Emo Soul**
**Anxiety Off Switch: Emergency Reset for a Fried Nervous System**
**The Energy Heist: How to Take Back Your Life from Drainers**
**Beyond the Bathroom: Rebuilding Your Social Life With DI**
**Coyote's Gift for Decision Makers**
**Ghoul-Goo: Spooky S'mores You'll Die For**
**Echoes in the Mirror: Scrying and Self-Destruction Magick**
**Thread and Thorn: Stitching Spells from Rural Cloth**
**The Mogwai Mind: Building Untouchable Wealth from Small Ideas**
**Be Your Own Guide: Trust Your Inner Compass**
**Hormones in Chaos: The Endocrine Puzzle of Diabetes Insipidus**
**ChronoCleanse: Detox Your Biological Timeline**
**The Limb You Hide Is the One That Saves You**
**Leaves, Bones, and Whisper Spells**
**The Dinosaur Mindset: Prehistoric Tactics for Modern Wealth**
**Clawing Back Control: A Bastet Method for Boundaries and Empowerment**
*Samhain Codes of the Forgotten*
**Orange Alchemy: The Autumnal Spellbook**
**Monster Within, Master Without**
**The Sigil That Sleeps**
**Hearthcraft: Yule Hearth Sigils and Winter Warmth Spells**
**Temple of the Purring Moon: Rituals from Bastet's Lineage**
**When the Earth Remembers Your Footsteps**
**Food for Mood: Eat to Heal Depression, Not Just Survive It**
**Witch of the Kudzu Vine: Southern Pagan Wealth Secrets**
**The Invisible Diagnosis: Advocating for Yourself With DI**

**The Coffin's Lullaby: Sleep Magick and Nightmares as Portals**
**Ashes of the Will: Rituals for Erasing the Self**
**The Fracture Rite: Shattering the Magickal Core**
**Funeral Candles: The Art of Emo Flame Magick**
**The Black Grimoire: A Blank Ritual for Writing in Absence**
**Phantom Thirst: A Halloween Survival Guide for Diabetes Insipidus**
**The Hollow Crown: Emo Royalty and Magick of the Outcast King**
**Sandpainting for the Soul**
**Falling Into Balance: Using the Extra Hour to Recalibrate Life**
**100 Southern Superstitions That Still Work**
**The DI Child: A Parent's Guide to Raising Hydrated, Happy Kids**
**The Jungle of Shame: Escaping the Hidden Lab of Doubt**
**The Witch's Toast: S'mores Spells and Creepy Confections**
**The Hoodoo Pantry: Spells from the Mason Jar**
**The Immortal Fortune: Secret Wealth Lessons from Captain Jack Harkness**
**The Specter's Embrace: Magick for Channeling Ghostly Lovers**
**Grateful Waters: A Thanksgiving Survival Guide for Diabetes Insipidus**
**The Seizure Gospel**
**Harvestbind: Autumn Sigils and Samhain Spells**
**Doctor Who: The Algorithmic Awakening**
**Silent Nights, Steady Waters: A Christmas Survival Guide for Diabetes Insipidus**
**The Extra Hour Effect: How One Hour Can Transform Everything**
**Blade Between the Breaths**
**Running with the Mountain Shadows**
**Echoes of the Failed Experiment – Becoming a Living Legacy**

**Swamp Witches & River Ghosts: Real Southern Hauntings**

**Cornbread Prophecies: Magical Recipes from a Southern Table**

**Doctor Who: The Signal in the Star**

**Bloomcraft: Spring Sigils and Equinox Enchantments**

**Vanisher: How to Disappear from the Internet Without Losing Your Life**

**The Ultimate Christmas Cookie Cookbook**

**The Unbreakable Parent: How to Mentally Survive Raising Kids in a Broken World**

**Time Debt: How to Reclaim the Hours You Didn't Know You Lost**

**One Month, One Million: Unconventional Cash Creation Tactics**

**Doctor Who: The Cyber Conversion Protocol**

**Black Friday Frenzy: The Art of Finding Hidden Online Deals**

**The Grimoire Buried Under the Apple Tree**

**Digital Couponing Masterclass: Your Step-by-Step Guide to Black Friday Savings**

**The Fire Inside the Flint**

**Shadows on the Ceiling: The Emo Guide to Astral Magick**

**The Bone-Eaters Beneath Us**

**Black Friday Bundle Blueprint: Creating Irresistible Product Packages for Maximum Sales**

**Thirteen Nights of Unbinding**

**Doctor Who: Engines of Influence**

**Pumpkin Spice Alchemy: Recipes of Fire and Frost**

**When Raptor Met Rexy: Prehistoric Lessons in Wild Romance**

**Oblivion's Candle: Burn the Path Behind You**

**Campfire Curses and Chocolate: A Halloween S'mores Grimoire**

**The Wallet That Wasn't Mine: Breaking Free from Inherited Scarcity**
**The Cola Zodiac: What Your Fizz Says About Your Fate**
**Frostfire Fortune: Unlocking Winter's Hidden Prosperity**
**Signal Jamming: Detox Your Brain from Info Overload**
**The Dust of the Forgotten Rite**
**The Golden Cat Sigils: Drawing Power in Bastet's Name**
**Mud Magick: The Prosperity of Getting Dirty**
**Savory Spicefall: Beyond the Pumpkin Pie**
**Pumpkin Spice Apothecary Kitchen**
**The Pumpkin Spice Economy: Turning Trends into Billions**
**The Ember Veil: 13 Nights of Fire Magick**
**Financial Freeze: When Earning Triggers Panic**
**The Gingerbread Alchemist: Sweet Recipes with a Twist**
**Biosynth Power: Programming Yourself from Scratch**
**Echoes from the Talking Circle**
**Truffle Alchemy: Fungus of Fortune**
**Spores of Power: The Truffle Witch's Handbook**
**Doctor Who: The Tower That Speaks**
**The Mycelium Veil: Truffle Magick Unbound**
**Broke But Ashamed: Healing the Shame Wound of Debt**
**The Evergreen Mind: Growth Through Winter Stillness**
**The Black Veil Truffle Rite**
**The Voice Beneath Symbols**
**Witchlight on the Bayou: Swamp Spells for Sovereignty**
**I Grew Up Poor and Now I Sabotage My Success**
**The Lantern of Hollow Souls**
**Shutdown Survival: A Citizen's Guide to Thriving When Government Stops**
**When Abundance Feels Like a Threat: Healing the Hidden Fears of Enough**
**The Scarecrow Grimoire**
**Owls of the October Veil**

**Candlewax and Curses: A Halloween Spellbook**

**Excavating the Inner Fossil – Transforming Fossilized Thoughtforms into Tools of Power**

**The Yule Witch's Spellbook: Magick for the Holiday Season**

**Haunted Christmas: Ghost Stories for Winter Nights**

**The Christmas Survival Guide: Thriving Through the Chaos**

**The Bone Orchard Rites**

**Haunted Commerce: The Ghost in the Marketplace**

**When Money Triggers the Inner Child**

**Silent Night with the Silence: A Christmas Thriller**

**The Lightning Crown: Living and Leading Through Seizures**

**TARDIS Tidings: Festive Stories from the Whoniverse**

**Autumn Reset: Slowing Down Without Falling Behind**

**The Trillion Dollar Soul: Rewriting the Currency of Reality**

**Truffle Eclipse Magick**

**Micro-Manifestations: Quick Magick That Works**

**5-Minute Rituals for Busy Witches**

**The Marshmallow Massacre: Halloween Treats with a Sinister Twist**

**Blood and Blackberry Thorns**

**Magickal Mornings: Rituals for a Blessed Christmas Day**

**Embers of the All-Hallows Fire**

**The Pumpkin Market Collapse**

**The Hour You Gained: Transforming Time Into Power**

**The Chamber Must Be Sealed: Mastering the Power of Controlled Access**

**The Cursed Manuscript of Petosiris**

**The Festive Hearth: Creating Holiday Traditions**

**Darkness Rising: Thriving as Nights Grow Longer**

**Harvesting Time: Turning the Year's End Into Your New Beginning**

**Petosiris and the 13th Zodiac Key**

**Wagewound: When Paychecks Become Identity Prisons**

**Walls That Watch**

**The Silent Feast: Rituals of Power in the Longest Night**

**The Distortus Legacy : Becoming a Deformed King in a Perfect World**

**The Hollow Masks**

**The Gratitude Furnace: Forging Gold from Thanks**

**Feast of Inner Gold: Eating for Energy and Enlightenment**

**Haunted Commerce: The Season of Spending Spirits**

**Fear Bonds: How Panic Creates Profit**

**Black Friday E-Commerce Playbook: Sales Tactics to Skyrocket Your Holiday Revenue**

**Budgeting for Black Friday: A Holiday Savings Planner**

**Haunting the Harvest Moon**

**The Warrior's Water: Emergency Preparedness for People With DI**

**The First Sip of the Year: A New Year's Survival Guide for Diabetes Insipidus**

**Doctor Who: The Thirteenth Node**

**The Unseen Struggle: Mental Health, Anxiety, and Chronic Thirst**

**The Hearth's Hidden Ledger: Counting Energies as Currency**

**The Gift Alchemist: Turning Any Offering Into Gold**

**The Papyrus of the Bound Spirit**

**The Magick of Leftovers: Transmutation in the Fridge**

**Frost and Fortune: Christmas Wealthcraft for the Modern Magus**

**Last-Minute Gifts: Creative Ideas on a Budget**

**10 Secrets to Surviving Holiday Crowds**

**The Witch's Dow Jones**

**The Witches' Graveyard Shift**

**Pumpkin Sigils: Carving Rites for Midnight Power**

**The Secret Shopper's Black Friday Guide: How to Get Early Access and VIP Deals**

Fever in the Foundation
The Neuralyzer Reset: Reprogram Your Morning Routine
Lightning Lessons of the White Painted Woman
The Enchanted Snowflake
The Magic Sip: Surviving Disney Parks with Diabetes Insipidus
The One Who Draws Through You
Santa's Secrets: A Magical Holiday Planner
Silent Bells, Loud Miracles: Self-Help for the Season of Stillness
The Sugar Spell Codex: Confectionary Magick of Christmas
Autumn Hexcraft: Fallen Leaves, Fallen Barriers
Sleep Like a Fortress: Build a Life Where Insomnia Can't Survive
Nowhere Was Ever Home
Christmas Under the Stars: A Celestial Holiday Guide
Rentproof: How to Never Be Evicted Again
Workless: Escape the 9-5 Without Being Broke
The Gilded Gift: A Wealth Altar for Christmas Morning
The Black Friday Grimoire
The Hollowing: Ceremonies of Spiritual Collapse
Doctor Who: The Nameless Signal
Where the Eagle Hides His Courage
The Dwarf Tyrant's Ascent: Claiming Power in a World of Giants
The Currency of the Dead: Trading with Spectral Bankers
The Icebound Witch: Survival and Magick in the Cold
The Emergency Money Mind: Constant Crisis, Zero Calm
Thirst & Roses: A Valentine's Survival Guide for Diabetes Insipidus
Springing Into Clarity: Mastering the Energy Shift of Daylight Saving
Speed of the Nanotyrant: Agile Strategies for Life's Hunt

**The 90-Day Reset: A Science-Backed Guide to Reinvent Yourself Before the New Year**

**The Coil of Thorns**

**Timegates Unleashed**

**Dopamine Fasting 2.0: Rewiring Your Brain in a World of Overstimulation**

**The Nanotyrannus Mutation: Embracing Your Differentiated Form**

**Unwritten January: How to Use the Blank Page of the Year to Re-Author Your Life**

**Feast of the Forgotten Spirits: Ancestor Magick for the Holidays**

**The Burnout Codex: A System for Thriving Beyond Stress**

**I Don't Deserve to Have Money**

**When the King Doesn't See You: The Shadow Predator's Guide**

**The Reset Ritual :A Guide to Shedding Last Year's Weight—Emotional and Physical—by Spring Cleaning Your Soul**

**Calendar Alchemy: Learn to Bend Time and Productivity around Your Natural Rhythms**

**The Mirror Contract: A One-Sentence Agreement with Yourself that Unlocks Real Change**

**The Nile Formula: Sacred Flow for Millionaire Minds**

**Forward Momentum: Productivity Rituals for the Lost Hour**

**Harvest Gold: Wealth Magick of Pumpkin Spice Commerce**

**The Magick of Christmas Lights: Illuminating Holiday Rituals**

**Cranberry Crown: Royal Self-Worth through Ritual Meals**

**Petosiris and the Worms of the Feathered Throne**

**The Evergreen Equation: Self-Help for Sustained Growth**

**The Rain Will Wash Us Away: Emo Weather Magick**

**Snowlight Shadows: Magick Under Frozen Stars**

**Doctor Who: Merger of Empires**

The Light Within the Feast: Magickal Wealth of Yuletide Flame

Momentum Machines: Small Habits Designed to Snowball into Unstoppable Forward Motion

Calm Spells: Magickal Solutions for Anxiety Relief

Santa's Final List: The Naughty Never Leave

The Mystic's Guide to Banishing Worry

The Silence Dividend: Turning Quiet Mornings into Compounding Growth All Year

Charmed Stillness: Rituals to Ease the Mind

Blood Spiral Ascension

The Vanishing Heart Invocation

Crystal Calm: Harnessing Stones for Anxiety

The Nano Tyrant Code: Strength in the Small Predator

The Energy Ledger: Accounting Methods for Vitality, Not Just Money

Snowglobe Mindset: Shake Up Your Thoughts, Settle Into Peace

The Weight of the Feather: Anubis's Codes for Soul Balance

Pocket Peppermint Power: Tiny Rituals for Big Holiday Energy

Shadowkeeper of the Golden Jackal: Anubis's Path to Energetic Protection

The Witch's Breath: Anxiety Relief Through Magickal Breathing

The Tiny Ember: Pocket Motivation for Cold Days

Stocking Sorcery: Mini Spells for Holiday Luck and Prosperity

Warm Hands, Steady Heart: Micro Grounding for Winter Anxiety

The Jackal's Lantern: Guide-Lights for Walking the Dark Path

Anubis's Silent Steps: Rituals for Stealth, Peace & Emotional Quiet

**The Bonewake Protocol**

**Extinction-Proof: How to Outlive Trends, Trauma, and Time**

**The Fourth Doctor: The Eccentric Wanderer**

**The Second Doctor: Chaos and Charm in the TARDIS (Patrick Troughton, 1966–1969)**

**The Third Doctor: Earthbound Defender of Time (Jon Pertwee, 1970–1974)**

**The First Doctor: Genesis of the Time Lord (William Hartnell, 1963–1966)**

**The Fourth Doctor: The Eccentric Wanderer** *(Tom Baker, 1974–1981)*

**The Fifth Doctor: Elegance and Empathy (Peter Davison, 1982–1984)**

**The Sixth Doctor: A Kaleidoscope of Conflict (Colin Baker, 1984–1986)**

**The Seventh Doctor: The Strategist of Shadows (Sylvester McCoy, 1987–1989)**

**The Eighth Doctor: A Time Lord's Renaissance (Paul McGann, 1996)**

**The War Doctor: A Time Lord's Burden (John Hurt, 2013)**

**The Ninth Doctor: The Healer of Worlds**
*(Christopher Eccleston, 2005)*

**The Tenth Doctor: The Lonely Hero (David Tennant, 2005–2010)**

**The Eleventh Doctor: The Madman in a Box (Matt Smith, 2010–2013)**

**The Twelfth Doctor: The Rebel with a Cause (Peter Capaldi, 2013–2017)**

*The Thirteenth Doctor: Breaking the Mold*
**(Jodie Whittaker, 2017–2022)**

**The Fourteenth Doctor: A New Beginning (David Tennant, 2022–2023)**

*The Fifteenth Doctor: Rewriting the Stars*
(Ncuti Gatwa, 2023–2025)

**Santa's Shortcut to Success: Micro Habits for a Better New Year**

**The Midnight Cocoa Manifesto: Comfort Rituals for Hard Nights**

**Why I Can't Save: Trauma Blocks to Financial Planning**

*Dino Brain, Mega Goals: Rewire Yourself for Savage Success.*

**Jurassic Profit: Unearth Your Inner Millionaire Fossil**

**Scales & Softness: Dating with Dino Heart**

*Carnotaurus Dreams.*

*Red Willow Thinking.*

**Reindeer Resilience: How to Keep Going When You're Exhausted**

**Candlewick Courage: Lighting Strength in Dark Seasons.**

**Elf-Mode Focus: Fast Attention Fixes for Busy Seasons**

**Futureproof Feelings: Emotional Skill-Building for Resilience No Matter What the New Year Brings**

**The 90-Day Rewire: Transform Your Neural Pathways Before Spring Blooms**

**Jolly Rich: Christmas Micro-Money Magick for Fast Prosperity.**

**Gingerbread Gratitude: Mini Practices for a Happier Holiday**

**Trauma-Spending: When Money Becomes a Drug**

**Goal Skeletons: Build Minimalist Frameworks for Resolutions That Last**

**The Snarl Strategy: Growling Back at a World That Silenced You**

**The Hourglass Reset: Reclaiming What the Clock Took**

**Yule Claw: Dino Rites of Light in the Darkness**

**Sacred Circles: Grounding Rituals for Anxious Souls**

**Clockstopper's Gut: Rebuilding the Core of Time**

**Winterfire Drive: Harness the Cold Season's Stillness to Ignite Deep Motivation**

**The 5-Minute Productivity Hack: Small Steps to Big Results**

**Light Ascending: A Self-Help Guide to Longer Days**

**Inner Economy: Trade Self-Doubt for Confidence Like a High-Value Currency**

**Simple Success: Decluttering Your Life for Better Results**

**The Resilient Mind: Thriving in Tough Times**

**The 2026 Playbook: Mastering the Year Ahead**

**The Spring Sleep Solution: Conquering Fatigue After Time Change.**

**The Hormonal Compass: Navigate Back to Your Youth**

**Golden Vision: Eating for Your Eye Color with the Power of Ghee**

**Lionhearted Love: Strength in Relationships**

**MiB Mindset: Think Like a Cosmic Agent**

**The Ladder of Small Wins: Climb Out of Stagnation by Stacking Micro-Victories**

*The Momentum Hour: Gaining More in Less Time.*

**The Year of You: A Self-Help Blueprint for Unapologetic Self-Ownership**

***The Dust That Watches You Back.***

**The Astral Parent**

Shadow of the King: The Nanotyrannus Parable

**Tiny Tidings of Triumph: Small Wins That Change Your Life**

**Dwarf Tyrant Rising: When You're the One They Overlook**

**The Bank Account Mirror: Healing How You See Yourself Through Money**

**Cretaceous Black**

**When Love Costs Too Much: Romantic Triggers and Financial Wounds**

**Dream-Eater's Guide to Wealth**

**Unzipped Reality: The Jacket That Opens Portals**

**The Power of No: How to Set Boundaries and Get Rich**

**Keeper of the Desert Veil: Anubis's Teachings on Illusion & Truth**

**Redacted Stargates: Stories the SGC Buried**

**The Clock That Dripped Time**

**Doctor Who: The Silent Acquisition**

**Hairline Manifestation: Unlocking Power at the Edge of Thought**

**Cash-Eater Crickets: How Insects Predict Economic Collapse**

**Dead Pet Whisperer: Grief Alchemy from the Other Side**

**The Love Algorithm Is Broken: Hack Romance Before It Hacks You**

**The Rite of the 8-Limbed Seal**

**Melt the Moon: A Fire Ritual to Reshape Emotion**

**Venomous Miracles: Healing Through the Poison Path**

Get Some Tarot cards: https://www.makeplayingcards.com/sell/apophis-occult-shop

Get some shirts: https://www.bonfire.com/store/apophis-shirt-emporium/

**Instagrams:**
**@apophis_enterprises,**
**@apophisbookemporium,**
**@apophisscardshop**
**Twitter: @apophisenterpr1**
**Tiktok:@apophisenterprise**
**Youtube: @sg1fan23477**
**Hive: @sg1fan23477**
**CheeLee: @SG1fan23477**

**Podcast: Apophis Chat Zone:** https://open.spotify.com/show/5zXbrCLEV2xzCp8ybrfHsk?si=fb4d4fdbdce44dec

**Newsletter:** https://apophiss-newsletter-27c897.beehiiv.com/

If you want to support me or see posts of other projects that I have come over to: **buymeacoffee.com/mpetchinskg**

I post there daily several times a day

Get your Dinowicca or Christmas themed digital products, especially Santa Raptor songs and other musics. Here: **https://sg1fan23477.gumroad.com**

Apophis Yuletide Digital has not only digital Christmas items, but it will have all things with Dinowicca as well as other Digital products.

Wealth Without Water

www.ingramcontent.com/pod-product-compliance
Lightning Source LLC
LaVergne TN
LVHW020235210926
848481LV00016B/2219

* 9 7 9 8 2 9 5 5 0 1 0 3 6 *